The Tale of Thidrandi and Thorhall

Original Text, Translations, and Word Lists

Translated by
Matthew Leigh Embleton

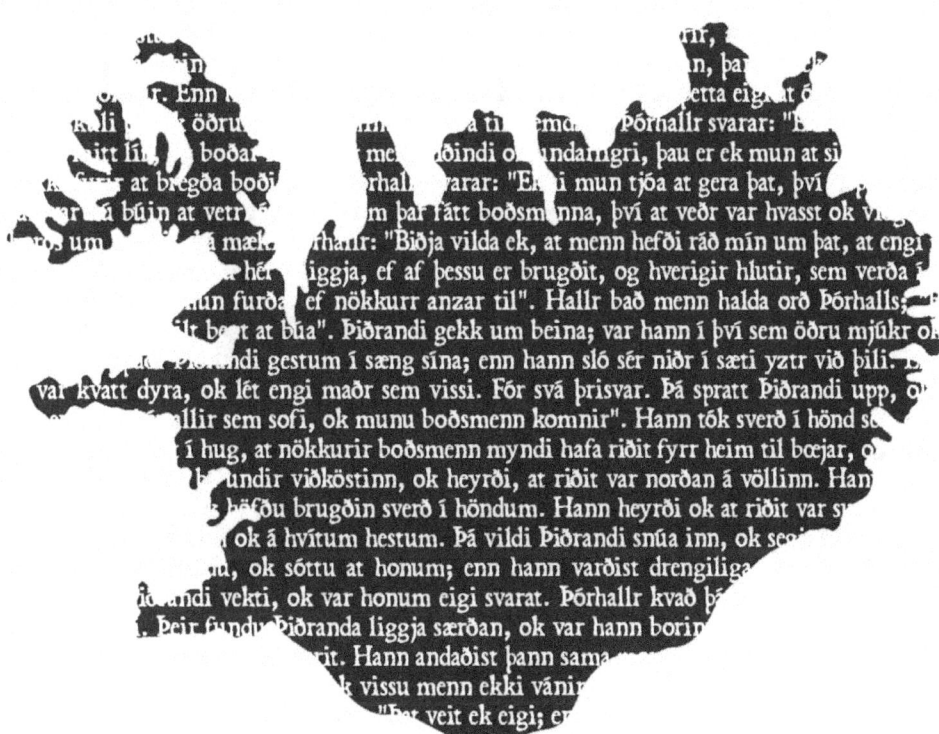

Copyright ©2025 Matthew Leigh Embleton. All rights reserved.

The Tale of Thidrandi and Thorhall

The Tale of Thiðrandi and Thórhall (*Old Norse*)..4
Word List *(Old Norse to English)*..13
Word List *(English to Old Norse)* 21
The Tale of Thiðrandi and Thórhall (*Old Icelandic*) 28
Word List *(Old Icelandic to English)*...37
Word List *(English to Old Icelandic)*...45
A Word Comparison of Old Norse and Old Icelandic Words 52

Cover: Old Norse text over an outline of Iceland. Author's design.

The original Old Norse and Old Icelandic texts are in the public domain.
These translations ©2022 Matthew Leigh Embleton
©2025 Matthew Leigh Embleton (This Edition)

Acknowledgments

I have long been fascinated by languages and history, and I am very grateful to the special people in my life who have supported and encouraged me in my work. Thank you for believing in me. You know who you are.

Introduction

Old Norse is a North Germanic language spoken by inhabitants of Scandinavia from about the 7th to the 15th centuries. Old Icelandic is a variety of Old West Norse that emerged during the Norse settlement of Iceland in the second half of the 9th century. The rich tradition of Icelandic literature survived by oral tradition over several centuries before being written down in the 13th Century. The Tale of Thiðrandi and Thórhall (*Þiðranda þáttr ok Þórhalls*) is one of the many Tales of Icelanders or *Íslendingaþættir*. The word '*þáttr*' (plural: '*þættir*') translates as a strand of rope or a yarn, comparable to the word 'yarn' in English sometimes used to refer to a story.

This book contains:
- The Tale of Thiðrandi and Thórhall (*Þiðranda þáttr ok Þórhalls*) (Old Norse Version)
- An Old Norse to English Word List
- An English to Old Norse Word List
- The Tale of Thiðrandi and Thórhall (*Þiðranda þáttr ok Þórhalls*) (Old Icelandic Version)
- An Old Icelandic to English Word List
- An English to Old Icelandic Word List
- A Word Comparison of Old Norse and Old Icelandic words

The texts are presented in their original form, with a literal word-for-word line-by-line translation, and a Modern English translation, all side-by-side. In this way, it is possible to see and feel how the worked and how it has evolved. This book is designed to be of use and interest to anyone with a passion for the Old Norse or Old Icelandic language, Norse history, or languages and history in general.

The Tale of Thiðrandi and Thórhall (*Old Norse*)

Old Norse	Literal	English
1	**1**	**1**
Þórhallr hét maðr norrœnn;	Thorhall was-named a-man northern;	There was a nordic man named Thorhall.
hann kom út til Íslands á dögum Hákonar jarls Sigurðarsonar.	he came out to Iceland in the-days-of Hakon the-earl Sigurdson.	He came out to Iceland in the days of earl Hakon Sigurdson.
Hann tók land í Sýrlœkjarósi, ok bjó á Hörgslandi.	He took land in Syrlaekjaros, and settled at Horgsland.	He took land in Syrlaekjaros and settled at Horgsland.
Þórhallr var fróðr maðr ok mjök framsýnn, ok var kallaðr Þórhallr spámaðr.	Thorhall was a-wise man and much far-sighted, and was called Thorhall the-Seer.	Thorhall was a wise man and very far-sighted, and he was called Thorhall the Seer
Þórhallr spámaðr bjó þá á Hörgslandi, er Síðu-Hallr bjó at Hofi í Álftafirði, ok var með þeim hin mesta vinátta.	Thorhall the-Seer settled then at Horgsland, when Sidu-Hall settled at Hof in Alftafjord, and was with them the most friendship.	Thorhall the Seer then settled at Horgsland when Sidu-Hall settled at Hof in Alftafjord and between them was the best friendship.
Gisti Hallr á Hörgslandi hvert sumar, er hann reið til þings.	Guested Hall at Horgsland each summer, as he rode to the-assembly.	Hall was a guest at Horgsland each summer as he ridden to the assembly.
Þórhallr fór ok oft til heimboða austr þangat, ok var þar löngum.	Thorhall travelled also often to home-invitation east from-there, and was there long.	Thorhall also travelled by invitation to the east and spent a long time there.
Sonr Halls hinn elzti hét Þiðrandi;	Son Hall's the eldest was-named Thidrandi;	Hall's eldest son was named Thidrand.
hann var manna vænstr ok efniligastr;	he was a-man handsome and promising;	He was a handsom and promising man.
unni Hallr honum mest allra sona sinna.	loved Hall him the-most of-all sons his.	Hall loved him the most of all his sons.
Þiðrandi fór landa í milli, þegar hann hafði aldr til.	Thidrandi travelled the-lands in between, once he had age to.	Thidrand travelled between lands as soon as he was old enough.

The Tale of Thiðrandi and Thórhall (Old Norse)

Old Norse	Literal	English
Hann var hinn vinsælasti, hvar sem hann kom, því at hann var hinn mesti atgervismaðr, lítillátr ok blíðr við hvert barn.	He was most endearing, where that he came, for that he was the most accomplished, modest and gentle with every child.	He was most endearing wherever he came, for he was the most accomplished but modest, and gentle with every man and child.
Þat var eitt sumar, at Hallr bauð Þórhalli vin sínum austr þangat, þá er hann reið af þingi.	It was one summer, that Hall invited Thorhall friend his east from-there, then when he was-riding from the-assembly.	It happened one summer that Hall invited Thorhall his friend to the east when he was riding home from the assembly.
Þórhallr fór austr nökkuru síðar enn Hallr, ok tók Hallr við honum sem jafnan með hin mesta blíðskap.	Thorhall travelled east sometime later than Hall, and took Hall with him as usual with the greatest kindness.	Thorhall travelled east sometime later than Hall, and Hall received him with with the greatest kindness as usual.
Dvaldist Þórhallr þar um sumarit, ok sagði Hallr, at hann skyldi eigi fyrri fara heim enn lokit væri haustboði.	Dwelled Thorhall there about summer, and said Hall, that he should not before travel home than ended the-home autumn-feast.	Thorhall dwelled there over the summer and Hall said that he should not travel home before the autumn feast had ended.

2

Þat sumar kom Þiðrandi út í Berufirði.	That summer came Thidrandi out to Berufjord.	That summer Thidrand came out to Berufjord.
Þá var hann átján vetra.	Then was he eighteen winters.	Then he was 18 winters old.
Fór hann heim til föður síns.	Travelled he home to father his.	He travelled home to his father.
Dáðust menn þá enn mjök at honum sem oft áðr, ok lofuðu atgervi hans; enn Þórhallr spámaðr þagði jafnan, þá er menn lofuðu hann mest.	Admired people then as much of him as often before, and praised deeds his; but Thorhall the-Seer silent always, then when people praised him the-most.	People admired him as much as before and praised his deeds, but Thorhall the Seer was always silent when people praised him the most.
Þá spurði Hallr, hví þat sætti,	Then asked Hall, what the reason,	Then Hall asked what the reason was for this:
"er þú leggr svá fátt til um hagi sonar míns Þiðranda? því at mér þykkir þat merkilegt, er þú mælir, Þórhallr", segir hann.	"are you suggesting so little to about health son mine Thidrandi? because that I think it remarkable, that-which you say, Thorhall", said he.	"because I think that whatever you say Thorhall is always remarkable to me", he said.
Þórhallr svaraði:	Thorhall answered:	Thorhall answered:

The Tale of Thiðrandi and Thórhall (Old Norse)

Old Norse	Literal	English
"Eigi gengr mér þat til þess, at mér mislíki nökkurr hlutr við hann eðr þik, eðr ek sjái síðr enn aðrir menn, at hann er hinn merkilegasti maðr, heldr berr hitt til, at margir verða til at lofa hann, ok hefir hann marga hluti til þess, þó at hann virði sik lítils sjálfr.	"Not goes to-me that to this, that I mislike some part with him or you, or-that I see less than other people, that he is the-most remarkable man, but bears others to, that many become until to praise him, and has he many things to this, although that he values himself little of-himself.	"It does not occur to me that I dislike anything about him or you, or that I see less than other men that he is the most remarkable man, but rather that many will praise him and he has many things to do with it, although he values himself little.
Kann þat vera, at hans njóti eigi lengi, ok mun þér þá œrin eftirsjá at um son þinn svá vel mannaðan, þó at eigi lofi allir menn fyrir þér hans atgervi".	Can it be, that he enjoys not for-long, and should you then mad look-back that about son yours so well manned, though that not praise all people for to-you his deeds".	It may be that he will not enjoy it for long, and then you will regret that your son is so well mannered, even though not all people praise you for his deeds".
Enn er á leið sumarit tók Þórhallr mjök at ógleðjast.	When was that passed summer took Thorhall much to ungladness.	When that summer was passed, Thorhall took much sadness.
Hallr spurði, hví þat sætti.	Hall asked, what the reason.	Hall asked what the reason was.
Þórhallr svarar:	Thorhall answered:	Thorhall answered:
"Illt hygg ek til haustboðs þessa, er hér skal vera, því at mér býðr þat fyrir, at spámaðr mun vera drepinn at þessi veizlu".	"Ill think I to autumn-harvest this, that here shall be, for to me invited it for, that a-seer shall be killed at this feast".	"I think evil of this autumn invitation which is to be here, for it offers me that a prophet will be killed at this feast".
"Þar kann ek at gera grein á", segir bóndi;	"Here can I that make explanation of", said the-farmer;	"I can explain that," said the farmer.
"ek á uxa einn, tíu vetra gamlan, þann er ek kalla spámann, því at hann er spakari enn flest naut önnur.	"I have ox one, ten winters old, that which I call the-Seer, because that he is wiser than most bulls others.	"I have a ten-year-old ox, whom I call the Prophet, for he is wiser than most other bulls.

The Tale of Thiðrandi and Thórhall (Old Norse)

Old Norse	Literal	English
Enn hann gkal drepa at haustboðinu, ok þarf þik þetta eigi at ógleðja, því at ek ætla, at þessi mín veizla sem aðrar skuli þér ok öðrum vinum mínum verða til sœmdar".	But he shall be-killed at autumn-feast, and need you this not be saddened, because that I suppose, that this my feast as others shall you and other friends mine be to honour".	But he will be killed at the autumn feast, and you need not be saddened because of this, for I think that this feast of mine, as well as others, will be an honour to you and to my other friends".
Þórhallr svarar:	Thorhall answered:	Thorhall answered:
"Ek fann þetta ok eigi af því til, at ek væra hræddr um mitt líf, ok boðar mér fyrir meiri tíðindi ok undarligri, þau er ek mun at sinni eigi upp kveða".	"I found this and not of because to, that I was scared about my life, and proclaims to-me for greater tidings and stranger, than is I may to mind not up speak".	"I found this not because I was afraid of my life, but because it proclaims to me more tidings and stranger ones that I have a mind not to speak up about".
Hallr mælti:	Hall said:	Hallur said:
"Þá er ok ekki fyrir at bregða boði því".	"Then is and not for that break to-break therefore".	"Then there is no way to break the offer".
Þórhallr svarar:	Thorhall answered:	Þórhallur answered:
"Ekki mun tjóa at gera þat, því at þat mun fram ganga sem ætlat er".	"Not would that be that the-matter, therefore that it should from going as intended be".	"It will not do in this matter because it will go as intended".

3

Veizlan var nú búin at vetrnóttum.	The-feast was prepared that winter-night.	The feast was prepared for the winter nights.
Kom þar fátt boðsmanna, því at veðr var hvasst ok viðgerðarmikit.	Came there few invited-men, because the weather was stormy and widely-made-much.	Few of the invited people came because the weather was stormy and difficult to travel in.
Enn er menn settust tilborðs um kveldit, þá mælti Þórhallr:	When were the-people sat to-the-tables about evening, then spoke Thorhall:	When the people sat at the tables in the evening then Thorhall spoke:

The Tale of Thiðrandi and Thórhall (Old Norse)

Old Norse	Literal	English
"Biðja vilda ek, at menn hefði ráð mín um þat, at engi maðr komi hér út á þessi nótt, því at mikil mein munu hér á liggja, ef af þessu er brugðit, og hverigir hlutir, sem verða í bendingum, gefi menn eigi gaum at, því at illu mun furða, ef nökkurr anzar til".	"Ask will I, that people have advice mine about it, that no man comes here outside on this night, for that much harm shall here to lay, if of this is broken, and whatever things, which happen as signs, give people not heed to, for that evil shall follow, if anyone responds to".	"I wish to ask that people hear my advice that no man goes outside on this night, for there shall be much harm if this is broken and whatever things people might see as signs are to be given no heed to, for evil shall follow if anyone answers".
Hallr bað menn halda orð Þórhalls;	Hall asked people hold words Thorhall's;	Hall asked people to hold to Thorhall's words:
"því at þau rjúfast ekki", segir hann,	"because that they break not", said he,	"because they will not break", he said,
"ok er um heilt bezt at búa".	"and is about wholly best to prepare".	"and it will be best to be wholly prepared".
Þiðrandi gekk um beina;	Thidrandi went about assisting;	Thidrand went about assisting.
var hann í því sem öðru mjúkr ok lítillátr.	was he as then as-in other-things humble and modest.	He was as in other things humble and modest.
Enn er menn gengu at sofa, þá skipaði Þiðrandi gestum í sæng sína; enn hann sló sér niðr í sæti yztr við þili.	But when people went to sleep, then directed Thidrandi guests to bed his; but he laid-out himself down on a-bench outer with wall.	But when people went to sleep Thidrand directed guests to his bed and he laid himself down on a bench at the outermost wall.
Enn er flestir menn váru sofnaðir, þá var kvatt dyra, ok lét engi maðr sem vissi.	When that most people were sleeping, then was summons at-the-door, and had no man as-if knew.	When most people were asleep there was a summons at the door, but no man acted as if they knew of it.
Fór svá þrisvar.	Came so three-times.	It came three times.
Þá spratt Þiðrandi upp, ok mælti:	Then sprang Thidrandi up, and spoke:	Then Thidrand sprang up and spoke:
"Þetta er skömm mikil, er menn láta hér allir sem sofi, ok munu boðsmenn komnir".	"This is a-shame great, that people let here all who sleep, and shall-be invited-men coming".	"This is a great shame that the people here are asleep and these must be guests coming".
Hann tók sverð í hönd sér, ok gekk út;	He took sword in hand his, and went out;	He took his sword in his hand and went out.
hann sá engan mann.	he saw no person.	He saw no person.

The Tale of Thiðrandi and Thórhall (Old Norse)

Old Norse	Literal	English
Honum kom þá þat í hug, at nökkurir boðsmenn myndi hafa riðit fyrr heim til bœjar, ok riðit síðan aftr í móti þeim, er seinna riðu,	To-him came then that a thought, that some invited-men would have rode for the-house to the-town, and rode afterwards back to meet them, that later rode,	A thought came to him that some guests would have ridden to the house and then back to the town to meet those who had ridden behind them arriving later.
Hann gekk þá undir viðköstinn, ok heyrði, at riðit var norðan á völlinn.	He went then under the-wood-pile, and heard, that riding was north into the-field.	He walked under the wood pile and heard the sound of riding coming from the north into the field.
Hann sá, at þat varu konur níu, ok allar í svörtum klæðum, ok höfðu brugðin sverð í höndum.	He saw, that it was women nine, and all in black clothes, and had drawn-out swords in hand.	He saw that there were nine women and they were all in black clothes and had drawn swords in their hands.
Hann heyrði ok at riðit var sunnan á völlinn,	He heard also that riding was from-the-south into the-field,	He also heard the sound of riding coming from the south into the field.
þar váru ok níu konur, allar í ljósum klæðum ok á hvítum hestum.	there were also nine women, all in bright clothes and on white horses.	There were also nine women, all in bright clothes and on white horses.
Þá vildi Þiðrandi snúa inn, ok segja mönnum sýnina; enn þá bar at konurnar fyrr, hinar svartklæddu, ok sóttu at honum; enn hann varðist drengiliga.	Then willed Thidrandi to-return inside, and say-to the-men this-sight; but then bore to the-women before, the black-clothes, and set-about to him; and he defended bravely.	Then Thidrand wished to return inside and tell the men of what he had seen, but then the women in the black clothes came upon him first and set about him, and he defended himself bravely.
Enn langri stundu síðar vaknaði Þórhallr, ok spurði, hvárt Þiðrandi vekti, ok var honum eigi svarat.	Then a-long while later woke Thorhall, and asked, whether Thidrandi awoke, and was he not answered.	A long while later Thorhall woke and asked whether Thidrand was awake but he was not answered.
Þórhallr kvað þá mundu of seinat.	Thorhall cried then would-be too-late.	Thorhall cried out that it would be too late.

4

Var þá út gengit;	Were they out going;	They went outside.

The Tale of Thiðrandi and Thórhall (Old Norse)

Old Norse	Literal	English
var á tunglskin ok frostviðri.	was it moonlight and frosty.	It was moonlight and frosty.
Þeir fundu Þiðranda liggja særðan, ok var hann borinn inn.	They found Thidrandi lying wounded, and was he carried inside.	They found Thidrand lying wounded and was he carried inside.
Ok er menn höfðu orð við hann, sagði hann þetta allt, sem fyrir hann hafði borit.	And when people had words with him, told he this all, that before he had bore.	And when the people had gotten word from him, he told them all that had happened before.
Hann andaðist þann sama morgun í lýsing, ok var lagðr í haug at heiðnum sið.	He died that same morning at daybreak, and was laid in a-mound as heathen tradition.	He died that same morning at daybreak and was laid in a mound as in the heathen tradition.
Síðan var haldit fréttum um mannaferðir, ok vissu menn ekki vánir óvina Þiðranda,	Later was held news about people's-travels, and knew people not the-hopes enemies-of Thidrandi,	Later there was news of peoples' travels and people did not know the hopes of Thidrand's enemies.
Hallr spurði Þórhall, hverju gegna myndi um þenna undarliga atburð.	Hall asked Thorhall, how going would about these strange events.	Hall asked Thorhall how these strange events would turn out.
Þórhallr svarar:	Thorhall answered:	Thorhall answered:
"Þat veit ek eigi; enn geta má ek til, at þetta hafi engar konur verit aðrar enn fylgjur yðrar frænda.	"That know I not; but guess may I to, that this have no women been other than followers your kinsmen.	"That I do not know, but I guess that these women can only have been followers of your kinsmen.
Get ek, at hér eftir komi siðaskifti, ok mun því næst koma siðr betri hingat til lands.	Guess I, that here after comes conversion, and should therefore next come a-custom better here to the-land.	I guess that there shall come a conversion, and there will be a better custom here to the land.
Ætla ek þær dísir yðrar, er fylgt hafa þessum átrúnaði, munu hafa vitat fyrir siðaskifti, ok þat, at þér munit verða þeim afhendir frændr.	Suppose I there spirits yours, were followers having this religion, would have known beforehand the-conversion, and it, that you shall come-to them rejected kinsmen.	I suppose that these spirits of you who have followed the old faith would have known beforehand about this conversion, and that they would be rejected by your kinsmen.
Nú munu þær eigi hafa því unat, at hafa engan skatt af yðr áðr, ok munu þær því hann haft hafa í sinn hlut;	Now shall they not have therefore liked, to have no tribute from you before, and would there that have in their lot;	Now they will not have liked to have had no tribute from you before and they would therefore have their lot.

The Tale of Thiðrandi and Thórhall (Old Norse)

Old Norse	Literal	English
enn hinar betri dísir mundri hafa viljat hjálpa honum, ok komust eigi við at svá búnu.	but the better spirits would will to-help him, and they-came not with to so good.	But the better spirits would have wished to help him, but they did not arrive in time.
Nú munut þér frændr þeira njóta, er þann hinn ókunna sið munut hafa, er þær boða fyrir ok fylgja".	Now shall you kinsmen of-them enjoy, which then shall have, what they preach for and follow".	Now your kinsmen shall enjoy the help of them by following what they preach for".

5

Nú boðaði þessi atburðr fyrir, sem Þórhallr sagði, ok margir hlutir þvílíkir, þann fagnaðartíma, sem eftir kom, at allsvaldandi Guði virðist at líta miskunnaraugum á þann lýð, er Ísland byggði, ok leysa þar fólk fyrir sína erindreka af löngum fjandans þrældómi, ok leiða síðan til samlags eilífrar erfðar sinna œskilegra sona, sem hann hefir fyrir heitit, alla þá, er honum vilja trúlega þjóna með staðfesti góðra verka;	Now foretold this event for, which Thorhall said, and many things like, that celebrated-time, which afterwards came, to omnipotent God seeming to look mercifully to that people, of Iceland settled, and redeemed that folk for their ambassadors of long damned slavery, and lead afterwards to union eternal inherited his desirable sons, whom he has before promised, all those, who him will truely serve with steadfast good works;	Now this event was foretold which Thorhall had said many things about, the celebrated time which came afterwards, an omnipotent god seeing and looking mercifully to the people that settled Iceland, redeeming the people from their ambassadors of long and damned slavery, leading afterwards to an eternal union, inherited by his desirable sons, that he has promised to all those who will truly serve him with steadfast good works.
svá ok eigi síðr sýndi óvinr alls mannkyns opinberliga í slíkum hlutum ok mörgum öðrum, þeim er í frásagnir eru fœrðir, hversu nauðigr hann lét laust sitt ránfengi ok þann lýð, er hann hafði áðr allan tíma haldit hertekinn í villuböndum sinna bölvuðu skurðgoða, þá er hann hvessti með slíkum áhlaupum sína grimdarfulla reiði á þeim, sem hann hafði vald yfir, sem hann vissi nálgast sína skömm ok makligan skaða síns herfangs.	so and no less it-seemed enemies all mankind publicly in such things and many others, they are of stories are told, how compelled he to-have without this robbery and that people, that he had before all time stayed captive of sins theirs cursed idols, then when he hissed with such raids his cruelty-full anger at them, which he had power over, which he knew approached their shame and make-like damage his war-takings.	So and it seemed no less that the enemies of all mankind publicly and in such things and many others, of which there are stories told of how they were compelled to abandon robbery, and the people that had before remained captive of the sins of their cursed idols when they hissed with such brutality and cruelty-full anger at those which they had power over, of which they knew they approached their shame, and the damage of their war-takings.

The Tale of Thiðrandi and Thórhall (Old Norse)

Old Norse	Literal	English
6	**6**	**6**
Enn Halli þótti svá mikit lát Þiðranda sonar síns, at hann undi eigi lengr at búa at Hofi;	But Hall thought so much had Thidrandi son his, that he on not longer to live at Hof;	But Halli thought so much of his son Thidrand's death that he could no longer live at Hof.
færði hann þá byggð sína til Þváttár.	brought he then settlement his to Thvatta.	He then moved his settlement to Thvatta.
Þat var einn tíma at Þváttá, þá er Þórhallr spámaðr var þar at heimboði með Halli, (at)	It was one time at Thvatta, then that Thorhall the-Seer was there at home-invitation with Hall, ()	There was a time at Thvatta when Thorhall the Seer was invited to stay with Hall.
Hallr lá í hvílugólfi ok Þórhallr í annarri rekkju; enn gluggr var á hvílugólfinu.	Hall lay in bed-closet and Thorhall in another bed; which window was on a-bed-closet.	Hall lay in a bed-closet and Thorhall in another bed-closet which had a window.
Ok einn morgin, er þeir vöktu báðir, þá brosti Þórhallr.	And one morning, when they woke both, then burst-out-laughing Thorhall.	And one morning they both woke and then Thorhall burst out laughing.
Hallr mælti:	Hall spoke:	Hall spoke:
"Hví brosir þú nú?"	"Why laughing are-you now?"	"Why are you laughing now?"
Þórhallr svarar:	Thorhall answered:	Thorhall answered:
"At því brosi ek, at margr hóll opnast, ok hvert kvikindi býr sinn bagga, bæði smá ok stór, ok gera fardaga".	"That because-of laughing am-I, that many hills they-open, and every creature prepares their bags, both small and great, and making moving-day".	"I am laughing because many hills are opening, and every creature prepares their bags, both small and great, and does their moving-day".
Ok litlu síðar urðu þau tíðindi, sem nú skal frá segja:	And little later came there the-news, that now shall from be-said:	And a little while later there came the news that shall now be said from.
(þ.e. kristniboð Þangbrands prests á Íslandi).	(i.e. christian-message Thangbrand priest in Iceland).	(i.e. The Christian message of Thangbrand the priest in Iceland).

Word List *(Old Norse to English)*

Old Norse	English
A, a	
aðrar	other, others
aðrir	other
af	from, from, of, of
afhendir	rejected
aftr	back
aldr	age
alla	all
allan	all
allar	all
allir	all, all
allra	of-all
alls	all
allsvaldandi	omnipotent
allt	all
andaðist	died
annarri	another
anzar	responds
at	as, at, at, be, be, of, that, that, the, to, to, 0
atburð	events
atburðr	event
atgervi	deeds
atgervismaðr	accomplished
austr	east, east
Á, á	
á	at, have, in, into, it, of, on, that, to
áðr	before
áhlaupum	raids
álftafirði	Alftafjord (place)
átján	eighteen
átrúnaði	religion
Æ, æ	
ætla	suppose
ætlat	intended
B, b	
bað	asked
báðir	both
bæði	both
bagga	bags
bar	bore
barn	child
bauð	invited
beina	assisting
bendingum	signs
berr	bears
berufirði	Berufjord (place)
betri	better
bezt	best
biðja	ask
bjó	settled
blíðr	gentle
blíðskap	kindness
boða	preach
boðaði	foretold
boðar	proclaims
boði	to-break
boðsmanna	invited-men
boðsmenn	invited-men
bœjar	the-town
bölvuðu	cursed
bóndi	the-farmer
borinn	carried
borit	bore
bregða	break
brosi	laughing
brosir	laughing
brosti	burst-out-laughing
brugðin	drawn-out
brugðit	broken
búa	live, prepare
búin	prepared
búnu	good
býðr	invited
byggð	settlement

Word List (Old Norse to English)

Old Norse	English
byggði	settled
býr	prepares

D, d

Old Norse	English
dáðust	admired
dísir	spirits
dögum	the-days-of
drengiliga	bravely
drepa	be-killed
drepinn	killed
dvaldist	dwelled
dyra	at-the-door

E, e

Old Norse	English
eðr	or, or-that
ef	if
efniligastr	promising
eftir	after, afterwards
eftirsjá	look-back
eigi	no, not
eilífrar	eternal
einn	one
eitt	one
ek	am-I, I
ekki	not
elzti	eldest
engan	no
engar	no
engi	no
enn	and, as, but, than, then, when, which
er	are, as, be, is, of, that, that-which, was, were, what, when, which, who
erfðar	inherited
erindreka	ambassadors
eru	are

F, f

Old Norse	English
fagnaðartíma	celebrated-time
fann	found
fara	travel
fardaga	moving-day
fátt	few, little
fjandans	damned
flest	most
flestir	most
föður	father
færði	brought
færðir	told
fólk	folk
fór	came, travelled
frá	from
frænda	kinsmen
frændr	kinsmen
fram	from
framsýnn	far-sighted
frásagnir	stories
fréttum	news
fróðr	a-wise
frostviðri	frosty
fundu	found
furða	follow
fylgja	follow
fylgjur	followers
fylgt	followers
fyrir	before, beforehand, for
fyrr	before, for
fyrri	before

G, g

Old Norse	English
gamlan	old
ganga	going
gaum	heed
gefi	give
gegna	going
gekk	went
gengit	going
gengr	goes
gengu	went
gera	make, making, that
gestum	guests
get	guess

14

Word List (Old Norse to English)

Old Norse	English
geta	guess
gisti	guested
gkal	shall
gluggr	window
góðra	good
grein	explanation
grimdarfulla	cruelty-full
guði	god

H, h

Old Norse	English
hafa	have, having, will
hafði	had
hafi	have
haft	that
hagi	health
hákonar	Hakon (name)
halda	hold
haldit	held, stayed
halli	Hall (name)
hallr	Hall (name)
halls	Hall's (name)
hann	he, him, 0
hans	he, his
haug	a-mound
haustboði	autumn-feast
haustboðinu	autumn-feast
haustboðs	autumn-harvest
hefði	have
hefir	has
heiðnum	heathen
heilt	wholly
heim	home, the-house
heimboða	home-invitation
heimboði	home-invitation
heitit	promised
heldr	but
hér	here
herfangs	war-takings
hertekinn	captive
hestum	horses
hét	was-named
heyrði	heard
hin	the
hinar	the

Old Norse	English
hingat	here
hinn	most, the, the-most, 0
hitt	others
hjálpa	to-help
hlut	lot
hluti	things
hlutir	things
hlutr	part
hlutum	things
höfðu	had
hofi	Hof (place)
hóll	hills
hönd	hand
höndum	hand
honum	he, him, to-him
hörgslandi	Horgsland (place)
hræddr	scared
hug	thought
hvar	where
hvárt	whether
hvasst	stormy
hverigir	whatever
hverju	how
hversu	how
hvert	each, every
hvessti	hissed
hví	what, why
hvílugólfi	bed-closet
hvílugólfinu	a-bed-closet
hvítum	white
hygg	think

I, i

Old Norse	English
illt	ill
illu	evil
inn	inside

Í, í

Old Norse	English
í	a, as, at, in, of, on, to
ísland	Iceland (place)
íslandi	Iceland (place)
íslands	Iceland (place)

Word List (Old Norse to English)

Old Norse	English
J, j	
jafnan	always, usual
jarls	the-earl
K, k	
kalla	call
kallaðr	called
kann	can
klæðum	clothes
kom	came
koma	come
komi	comes
komnir	coming
komust	they-came
konur	women
konurnar	the-women
kristniboð	christian-message
kvað	cried
kvatt	summons
kveða	speak
kveldit	evening
kvikindi	creature
L, l	
lá	lay
lagðr	laid
land	land
landa	the-lands
lands	the-land
langri	a-long
lát	had
láta	let
laust	without
leggr	suggesting
leið	passed
leiða	lead
lengi	for-long
lengr	longer
lét	had, to-have

Old Norse	English
leysa	redeemed
líf	life
liggja	lay, lying
líta	look
lítillátr	modest
lítils	little
litlu	little
ljósum	bright
lofa	praise
lofi	praise
lofuðu	praised
lokit	ended
löngum	long
lýð	people
lýsing	daybreak
M, m	
má	may
maðr	a-man, man
mælir	say
mælti	said, spoke
makligan	make-like
mann	person
manna	a-man
mannaðan	manned
mannaferðir	people's-travels
mannkyns	mankind
marga	many
margir	many
margr	many
með	with
mein	harm
meiri	greater
menn	people, the-people
mér	I, me, to-me
merkilegasti	remarkable
merkilegt	remarkable
mest	the-most
mesta	greatest, most
mesti	most
mikil	great, much
mikit	much
milli	between
mín	mine, my

Word List (Old Norse to English)

Old Norse	English
míns	mine
mínum	mine
miskunnaraugum	mercifully
mislíki	mislike
mitt	my
mjök	much
mjúkr	humble
mönnum	the-men
morgin	morning
mörgum	many
morgun	morning
móti	meet
mun	may, shall, should, would
mundri	would
mundu	would-be
munit	shall
munu	shall, shall-be, would
munut	shall
myndi	would

N, n

næst	next
nálgast	approached
nauðigr	compelled
naut	bulls
niðr	down
níu	nine
njóta	enjoy
njóti	enjoys
nökkurir	some
nökkurr	anyone, some
nökkuru	sometime
norðan	north
norrœnn	northern
nótt	night
nú	now, 0

O, o

of	too-late
oft	often
og	and
ok	also, and
opinberliga	publicly
opnast	they-open
orð	words

Ó, ó

ógleðja	saddened
ógleðjast	ungladness
ókunna	0
óvina	enemies-of
óvinr	enemies

Ö, ö

öðru	other-things
öðrum	other, others
önnur	others

Œ, œ

œrin	mad
œskilegra	desirable

P, p

prests	priest

R, r

ráð	advice
ránfengi	robbery
reið	rode, was-riding
reiði	anger
rekkju	bed
riðit	riding, rode
riðu	rode
rjúfast	break

Word List (Old Norse to English)

Old Norse	English
S, s	
sá	saw
sæng	bed
særðan	wounded
sæti	a-bench
sætti	reason
sagði	said, told
sama	same
samlags	union
segir	said
segja	be-said, say-to
seinat	0
seinna	later
sem	as, as-if, as-in, that, which, who, whom
sér	himself, his
settust	sat
sið	tradition, 0
síðan	afterwards, later
síðar	later
siðaskifti	conversion, the-conversion
siðr	a-custom
síðr	less
síðu-hallr	Sidu-Hall (name)
sigurðarsonar	Sigurdson (name)
sik	himself
sína	his, their
sinn	their
sinna	his, theirs
sinni	mind
síns	his
sínum	his
sitt	this
sjái	see
sjálfr	of-himself
skaða	damage
skal	shall
skatt	tribute
skipaði	directed
skömm	a-shame, shame
skuli	shall
skurðgoða	idols
skyldi	should

Old Norse	English
slíkum	such
sló	laid-out
smá	small
snúa	to-return
sœmdar	honour
sofa	sleep
sofi	sleep
sofnaðir	sleeping
son	son
sona	sons
sonar	son
sonr	son
sóttu	set-about
spakari	wiser
spámaðr	a-seer, the-Seer
spámann	the-Seer
spratt	sprang
spurði	asked
staðfesti	steadfast
stór	great
stundu	while
sumar	summer
sumarit	summer
sunnan	from-the-south
svá	so
svaraði	answered
svarar	answered
svarat	answered
svartklæddu	black-clothes
sverð	sword, swords
svörtum	black
sýndi	it-seemed
sýnina	this-sight
sýrlœkjarósi	Syrlaekjaros (place)
T, t	
tíðindi	the-news, tidings
til	to, until
tilborðs	to-the-tables
tíma	time
tíu	ten
tjóa	that
tók	took
trúlega	truely

Word List (Old Norse to English)

Old Norse	English
tunglskin	moonlight

Þ, þ

Old Norse	English
þ.e	i.e.
þá	then, they, those
þær	there, they
þagði	silent
þangat	from-there
þangbrands	Thangbrand (name)
þann	that, that, then
þar	here, that, there
þarf	need
þat	it, that, the, the, the-matter
þau	than, there, they
þegar	once
þeim	them, they
þeir	they
þeira	of-them
þenna	these
þér	to-you, you
þess	this
þessa	this
þessi	this
þessu	this
þessum	this
þetta	this
þiðranda	Thidrandi (name)
þiðrandi	Thidrandi (name)
þik	you
þili	wall
þingi	the-assembly
þings	the-assembly
þinn	yours
þjóna	serve
þó	although, though
þórhall	Thorhall (name)
þórhalli	Thorhall (name)
þórhallr	Thorhall (name)
þórhalls	Thorhall's (name)
þótti	thought
þrældómi	slavery
þrisvar	three-times
þú	are-you, you
þváttá	Thvatta (place)
þváttár	Thvatta (place)
því	because, because-of, for, then, therefore, 0
þvílíkir	like
þykkir	think

U, u

Old Norse	English
um	about
unat	liked
undarliga	strange
undarligri	stranger
undi	on
undir	under
unni	loved
upp	up
urðu	came
uxa	ox

Ú, ú

Old Norse	English
út	out, outside

V, v

Old Norse	English
vænstr	handsome
væra	was
væri	the-home
vaknaði	woke
vald	power
vánir	the-hopes
var	was, were
varðist	defended
varu	was
váru	were
veðr	weather
veit	know
veizla	feast
veizlan	the-feast
veizlu	feast
vekti	awoke
vel	well

Word List (Old Norse to English)

Old Norse	English
vera	be
verða	be, become, come-to, happen
verit	been
verka	works
vetra	winters
vetrnóttum	winter-night
við	with
viðgerðar-mikit	widely-made-much
viðköstinn	the-wood-pile
vilda	will
vildi	willed
vilja	will
viljat	0
villuböndum	sins
vin	friend
vinátta	friendship
vinsælasti	endearing
vinum	friends
virði	values
virðist	seeming
vissi	knew
vissu	knew
vitat	known
vöktu	woke
völlinn	the-field

Y, y

yðr	you
yðrar	your, yours
yfir	over
yztr	outer

Word List (English to Old Norse)

Word List *(English to Old Norse)*

English	*Old Norse*

A, a

English	*Old Norse*
a	*í*
a-bed-closet	*hvílugólfinu*
a-bench	*sæti*
about	*um*
accomplished	*atgervismaðr*
a-custom	*siðr*
admired	*dáðust*
advice	*ráð*
after	*eftir*
afterwards	*eftir, síðan*
age	*aldr*
Alftafjord (place)	*álftafirði*
all	*alla, allan, allar, allir, alls, allt*
a-long	*langri*
also	*ok*
although	*þó*
always	*jafnan*
a-man	*maðr, manna*
ambassadors	*erindreka*
am-I	*ek*
a-mound	*haug*
and	*enn, og, ok*
anger	*reiði*
another	*annarri*
answered	*svaraði, svarar, svarat*
anyone	*nökkurr*
approached	*nálgast*
are	*er, eru*
are-you	*þú*
as	*at, enn, er, í, sem*
a-seer	*spámaðr*
a-shame	*skömm*
as-if	*sem*
as-in	*sem*
ask	*biðja*
asked	*bað, spurði*
assisting	*beina*
at	*á, at, í*
at-the-door	*dyra*

English	*Old Norse*
autumn-feast	*haustboði, haustboðinu*
autumn-harvest	*haustboðs*
a-wise	*fróðr*
awoke	*vekti*

B, b

English	*Old Norse*
back	*aftr*
bags	*bagga*
be	*at, er, vera, verða*
bears	*berr*
because	*því*
because-of	*því*
become	*verða*
bed	*rekkju, sæng*
bed-closet	*hvílugólfi*
been	*verit*
before	*áðr, fyrir, fyrr, fyrri*
beforehand	*fyrir*
be-killed	*drepa*
Berufjord (place)	*berufirði*
be-said	*segja*
best	*bezt*
better	*betri*
between	*milli*
black	*svörtum*
black-clothes	*svartklæddu*
bore	*bar, borit*
both	*báðir, bæði*
bravely	*drengiliga*
break	*bregða, rjúfast*
bright	*ljósum*
broken	*brugðit*
brought	*fœrði*
bulls	*naut*
burst-out-laughing	*brosti*
but	*enn, heldr*

Word List (English to Old Norse)

English	Old Norse

C, c

English	Old Norse
call	*kalla*
called	*kallaðr*
came	*fór, kom, urðu*
can	*kann*
captive	*hertekinn*
carried	*borinn*
celebrated-time	*fagnaðartíma*
child	*barn*
christian-message	*kristniboð*
clothes	*klæðum*
come	*koma*
comes	*komi*
come-to	*verða*
coming	*komnir*
compelled	*nauðigr*
conversion	*siðaskifti*
creature	*kvikindi*
cried	*kvað*
cruelty-full	*grimdarfulla*
cursed	*bölvuðu*

D, d

English	Old Norse
damage	*skaða*
damned	*fjandans*
daybreak	*lýsing*
deeds	*atgervi*
defended	*varðist*
desirable	*œskilegra*
died	*andaðist*
directed	*skipaði*
down	*niðr*
drawn-out	*brugðin*
dwelled	*dvaldist*

E, e

English	Old Norse
each	*hvert*
east	*austr*
eighteen	*átján*
eldest	*elzti*
endearing	*vinsælasti*
ended	*lokit*
enemies	*óvinr*
enemies-of	*óvina*
enjoy	*njóta*
enjoys	*njóti*
eternal	*eilífrar*
evening	*kveldit*
event	*atburðr*
events	*atburð*
every	*hvert*
evil	*illu*
explanation	*grein*

F, f

English	Old Norse
far-sighted	*framsýnn*
father	*föður*
feast	*veizla, veizlu*
few	*fátt*
folk	*fólk*
follow	*furða, fylgja*
followers	*fylgjur, fylgt*
for	*fyrir, fyrr, því*
foretold	*boðaði*
for-long	*lengi*
found	*fann, fundu*
friend	*vin*
friends	*vinum*
friendship	*vinátta*
from	*af, frá, fram*
from-there	*þangat*
from-the-south	*sunnan*
frosty	*frostviðri*

G, g

English	Old Norse
gentle	*blíðr*
give	*gefi*
god	*guði*
goes	*gengr*
going	*ganga, gegna, gengit*
good	*búnu, góðra*
great	*mikil, stór*

Word List (English to Old Norse)

English	Old Norse
greater	*meiri*
greatest	*mesta*
guess	*get, geta*
guested	*gisti*
guests	*gestum*

H, h

English	Old Norse
had	*hafði, höfðu, lát, lét*
Hakon (name)	*hákonar*
Hall (name)	*halli, hallr*
Hall's (name)	*halls*
hand	*hönd, höndum*
handsome	*vænstr*
happen	*verða*
harm	*mein*
has	*hefir*
have	*á, hafa, hafi, hefði*
having	*hafa*
he	*hann, hans, honum*
health	*hagi*
heard	*heyrði*
heathen	*heiðnum*
heed	*gaum*
held	*haldit*
here	*hér, hingat, þar*
hills	*hóll*
him	*hann, honum*
himself	*sér, sik*
his	*hans, sér, sína, sinna, síns, sínum*
hissed	*hvessti*
Hof (place)	*hofi*
hold	*halda*
home	*heim*
home-invitation	*heimboða, heimboði*
honour	*sœmdar*
Horgsland (place)	*hörgslandi*
horses	*hestum*
how	*hverju, hversu*
humble	*mjúkr*

I, i

English	Old Norse
I	*ek, mér*
i.e.	*þ.e*
Iceland (place)	*ísland, íslandi, íslands*
idols	*skurðgoða*
if	*ef*
ill	*illt*
in	*á, í*
inherited	*erfðar*
inside	*inn*
intended	*ætlat*
into	*á*
invited	*bauð, býðr*
invited-men	*boðsmanna, boðsmenn*
is	*er*
it	*á, þat*
it-seemed	*sýndi*

K, k

English	Old Norse
killed	*drepinn*
kindness	*blíðskap*
kinsmen	*frænda, frændr*
knew	*vissi, vissu*
know	*veit*
known	*vitat*

L, l

English	Old Norse
laid	*lagðr*
laid-out	*sló*
land	*land*
later	*seinna, síðan, síðar*
laughing	*brosi, brosir*
lay	*lá, liggja*
lead	*leiða*
less	*síðr*
let	*láta*
life	*líf*
like	*þvílíkir*
liked	*unat*

Word List (English to Old Norse)

English	*Old Norse*	English	*Old Norse*
little	*fátt, lítils, litlu*	no	*eigi, engan, engar, engi*
live	*búa*	north	*norðan*
long	*löngum*	northern	*norrœnn*
longer	*lengr*	not	*eigi, ekki*
look	*líta*	now	*nú*
look-back	*eftirsjá*		
lot	*hlut*		
loved	*unni*		
lying	*liggja*		

M, m

O, o

English	*Old Norse*	English	*Old Norse*
mad	*œrin*	of	*á, af, at, er, í*
make	*gera*	of-all	*allra*
make-like	*makligan*	of-himself	*sjálfr*
making	*gera*	often	*oft*
man	*maðr*	of-them	*þeira*
mankind	*mannkyns*	old	*gamlan*
manned	*mannaðan*	omnipotent	*allsvaldandi*
many	*marga, margir, margr, mörgum*	on	*á, í, undi*
		once	*þegar*
may	*má, mun*	one	*einn, eitt*
me	*mér*	or	*eðr*
meet	*móti*	or-that	*eðr*
mercifully	*miskunnaraugum*	other	*aðrar, aðrir, öðrum*
mind	*sinni*	others	*aðrar, hitt, öðrum, önnur*
mine	*mín, míns, mínum*		
mislike	*mislíki*	other-things	*öðru*
modest	*lítillátr*	out	*út*
moonlight	*tunglskin*	outer	*yztr*
morning	*morgin, morgun*	outside	*út*
most	*flest, flestir, hinn, mesta, mesti*	over	*yfir*
		ox	*uxa*
moving-day	*fardaga*		
much	*mikil, mikit, mjök*		
my	*mín, mitt*		

N, n

P, p

English	*Old Norse*	English	*Old Norse*
need	*þarf*	part	*hlutr*
news	*fréttum*	passed	*leið*
next	*næst*	people	*lýð, menn*
night	*nótt*	people's-travels	*mannaferðir*
nine	*níu*	person	*mann*
		power	*vald*
		praise	*lofa, lofi*
		praised	*lofuðu*
		preach	*boða*
		prepare	*búa*
		prepared	*búin*

Word List (English to Old Norse)

English	*Old Norse*	English	*Old Norse*
prepares	*býr*	signs	*bendingum*
priest	*prests*	Sigurdson (name)	*sigurðarsonar*
proclaims	*boðar*	silent	*þagði*
promised	*heitit*	sins	*villuböndum*
promising	*efniligastr*	slavery	*þrældómi*
publicly	*opinberliga*	sleep	*sofa, sofi*
		sleeping	*sofnaðir*
		small	*smá*
		so	*svá*

R, r

English	*Old Norse*	English	*Old Norse*
		some	*nökkurir, nökkurr*
raids	*áhlaupum*	sometime	*nökkuru*
reason	*sætti*	son	*son, sonar, sonr*
redeemed	*leysa*	sons	*sona*
rejected	*afhendir*	speak	*kveða*
religion	*átrúnaði*	spirits	*dísir*
remarkable	*merkilegasti, merkilegt*	spoke	*mælti*
		sprang	*spratt*
responds	*anzar*	stayed	*haldit*
riding	*riðit*	steadfast	*staðfesti*
robbery	*ránfengi*	stories	*frásagnir*
rode	*reið, riðit, riðu*	stormy	*hvasst*
		strange	*undarliga*
		stranger	*undarligri*
		such	*slíkum*

S, s

English	*Old Norse*
suggesting	*leggr*
summer	*sumar, sumarit*
summons	*kvatt*
suppose	*ætla*
sword	*sverð*
swords	*sverð*
Syrlaekjaros (place)	*sýrlœkjarósi*

English	*Old Norse*
saddened	*ógleðja*
said	*mælti, sagði, segir*
same	*sama*
sat	*settust*
saw	*sá*
say	*mælir*
say-to	*segja*
scared	*hræddr*
see	*sjái*
seeming	*virðist*
serve	*þjóna*
set-about	*sóttu*
settled	*bjó, byggði*
settlement	*byggð*
shall	*gkal, mun, munit, munu, munut, skal, skuli*
shall-be	*munu*
shame	*skömm*
should	*mun, skyldi*
Sidu-Hall (name)	*síðu-hallr*

T, t

English	*Old Norse*
ten	*tíu*
than	*enn, þau*
Thangbrand (name)	*þangbrands*
that	*á, at, er, gera, haft, sem, þann, þar, þat, tjóa*
that-which	*er*
the	*at, hin, hinar, hinn, þat*
the-assembly	*þingi, þings*
the-conversion	*siðaskifti*

Word List (English to Old Norse)

English	Old Norse	English	Old Norse
the-days-of	dögum	time	tíma
the-earl	jarls	to	á, at, í, til
the-farmer	bóndi	to-break	boði
the-feast	veizlan	to-have	lét
the-field	völlinn	to-help	hjálpa
the-home	væri	to-him	honum
the-hopes	vánir	told	fœrðir, sagði
the-house	heim	to-me	mér
their	sína, sinn	took	tók
theirs	sinna	too-late	of
the-land	lands	to-return	snúa
the-lands	landa	to-the-tables	tilborðs
them	þeim	to-you	þér
the-matter	þat	tradition	sið
the-men	mönnum	travel	fara
the-most	hinn, mest	travelled	fór
then	enn, þá, þann, því	tribute	skatt
the-news	tíðindi	truely	trúlega
the-people	menn		
there	þær, þar, þau		
therefore	því		
these	þenna		

U, u

English	Old Norse
the-Seer	spámaðr, spámann
the-town	bœjar
the-women	konurnar
the-wood-pile	viðköstinn
they	þá, þær, þau, þeim, þeir
they-came	komust
they-open	opnast
Thidrandi (name)	Þiðranda, Þiðrandi
things	hluti, hlutir, hlutum
think	hygg, þykkir
this	sitt, þess, þessa, þessi, þessu, þessum, þetta

(continued)

English	Old Norse
under	undir
ungladness	ógleðjast
union	samlags
until	til
up	upp
usual	jafnan

V, v

English	Old Norse
values	virði

W, w

English	Old Norse
this-sight	sýnina
Thorhall (name)	Þórhall, Þórhalli, Þórhallr
Thorhall's (name)	Þórhalls
those	þá
though	þó
thought	hug, þótti
three-times	þrisvar
Thvatta (place)	Þváttá, Þváttár
tidings	tíðindi

English	Old Norse
wall	þili
war-takings	herfangs
was	er, væra, var, varu
was-named	hét
was-riding	reið
weather	veðr
well	vel
went	gekk, gengu
were	er, var, váru

Word List (English to Old Norse)

English	Old Norse
what	*er, hví*
whatever	*hverigir*
when	*enn, er*
where	*hvar*
whether	*hvárt*
which	*enn, er, sem*
while	*stundu*
white	*hvítum*
who	*er, sem*
wholly	*heilt*
whom	*sem*
why	*hví*
widely-made-much	*viðgerðar-mikit*
will	*hafa, vilda, vilja*
willed	*vildi*
window	*gluggr*
winter-night	*vetrnóttum*
winters	*vetra*
wiser	*spakari*
with	*með, við*
without	*laust*
woke	*vaknaði, vöktu*
women	*konur*
words	*orð*
works	*verka*
would	*mun, mundri, munu, myndi*
would-be	*mundu*
wounded	*særðan*

Y, y

you	*þér, þik, þú, yðr*
your	*yðrar*
yours	*þinn, yðrar*

The Tale of Thiðrandi and Thórhall (*Old Icelandic*)

Old Icelandic	Literal	English
1	**1**	**1**
Þórhallur hét maður norrænn.	Thorhall was-named a-man northern.	There was a nordic man named Thorhall.
Hann kom út til Íslands á dögum Hákonar jarls Sigurðarsonar.	He came out to Iceland in the-days-of Hakon the-earl Sigurdson.	He came out to Iceland in the days of earl Hakon Sigurdson.
Hann tók land í Sýrlækjarósi og bjó á Hörgslandi.	He took land in Syrlaekjaros and settled at Horgsland.	He took land in Syrlaekjaros and settled at Horgsland.
Þórhallur var fróður maður og mjög framsýnn og var kallaður Þórhallur spámaður.	Thorhall was a-wise man and much far-sighted and was called Thorhall the-Seer.	Thorhall was a wise man and very far-sighted, and he was called Thorhall the Seer
Þórhallur spámaður bjó þá á Hörgslandi er Síðu-Hallur bjó að Hofi í Álftafirði og var með þeim hin mesta vinátta.	Thorhall the-Seer settled then at Horgsland when Sidu-Hall settled at Hof in Alftafjord and was with them the most friendship.	Thorhall the Seer then settled at Horgsland when Sidu-Hall settled at Hof in Alftafjord and between them was the best friendship.
Gisti Hallur á Hörgslandi hvert sumar er hann reið til þings.	Guested Hall at Horgsland each summer as he rode to the-assembly.	Hall was a guest at Horgsland each summer as he ridden to the assembly.
Þórhallur fór og oft til heimboða austur þangað og var þar löngum.	Thorhall travelled also often to home-invitation east from-there and was there long.	Thorhall also travelled by invitation to the east and spent a long time there.
Sonur Halls hinn elsti hét Þiðrandi.	Son Hall's the eldest was-named Thidrandi.	Hall's eldest son was named Thidrand.
Hann var manna vænstur og efnilegastur.	He was a-man handsome and promising.	He was a handsom and promising man.
Unni Hallur honum mest allra sona sinna.	Loved Hall him the-most of-all sons his.	Hall loved him the most of all his sons.
Þiðrandi fór landa í milli þegar hann hafði aldur til.	Thidrandi travelled the-lands in between once he had age to.	Thidrand travelled between lands as soon as he was old enough.

The Tale of Thiðrandi and Thórhall (Old Icelandic)

Old Icelandic	Literal	English
Hann var hinn vinsælasti hvar sem hann kom því að hann var hinn mesti atgervimaður, lítillátur og blíður við hvert barn.	He was most endearing where that he came for that he was the most accomplished, modest and gentle with every child.	He was most endearing wherever he came, for he was the most accomplished but modest, and gentle with every man and child.
Það var eitt sumar að Hallur bauð Þórhalli vin sínum austur þangað þá er hann reið af þingi.	It was one summer that Hall invited Thorhall friend his east from-there then when he was-riding from the-assembly.	It happened one summer that Hall invited Thorhall his friend to the east when he was riding home from the assembly.
Þórhallur fór austur nokkuru síðar en Hallur og tók Hallur við honum sem jafnan með hinum mesta blíðskap.	Thorhall travelled east sometime later than Hall and took Hall with him as usual with the greatest kindness.	Thorhall travelled east sometime later than Hall, and Hall received him with with the greatest kindness as usual.
Dvaldist Þórhallur þar um sumarið og sagði Hallur að hann skyldi eigi fyrri fara heim en lokið væri haustboði.	Dwelled Thorhall there about summer and said Hall that he should not before travel home than ended the-home autumn-feast.	Thorhall dwelled there over the summer and Hall said that he should not travel home before the autumn feast had ended.
Það sumar kom Þiðrandi út í Berufirði.	That summer came Thidrandi out to Berufjord.	That summer Thidrand came out to Berufjord.
Þá var hann átján vetra.	Then was he eighteen winters.	Then he was 18 winters old.
Fór hann heim til föður síns.	Travelled he home to father his.	He travelled home to his father.
Dáðust menn þá enn mjög að honum sem oft áður og lofuðu atgervi hans en Þórhallur spámaður þagði jafnan þá er menn lofuðu hann mest.	Admired people then as much of him as often before and praised deeds his but Thorhall the-Seer silent always then when people praised him the-most.	People admired him as much as before and praised his deeds, but Thorhall the Seer was always silent when people praised him the most.
Þá spurði Hallur hví það sætti	Then asked Hall what the reason:	Then Hall asked what the reason was for this:
"því að mér þykir það merkilegt er þú mælir Þórhallur", segir hann.	"because that I think it remarkable that-which you say Thorhall", said he.	"because I think that whatever you say Thorhall is always remarkable to me", he said.
Þórhallur svaraði:	Thorhall answered:	Thorhall answered:

The Tale of Thiðrandi and Thórhall (Old Icelandic)

Old Icelandic	Literal	English
"Ekki gengur mér það til þess að mér mislíki nokkur hlutur við hann eða þig eða eg sjái síður en aðrir menn að hann er hinn merkilegasti maður heldur ber hitt til að margir verða til að lofa hann og hefir hann marga hluti til þess þó að hann virði sig lítils sjálfur.	"Not goes to-me that to this that I mislike some part with him or you or-that I see less than other people that he is the-most remarkable man but bears others to that many become until to praise him and has he many things to this although that he values himself little of-himself.	"It does not occur to me that I dislike anything about him or you, or that I see less than other men that he is the most remarkable man, but rather that many will praise him and he has many things to do with it, although he values himself little.
Kann það vera að hans njóti eigi lengi og mun þér þá ærin eftirsjá að um son þinn svo vel mannaðan þó að eigi lofi allir menn fyrir þér hans atgervi".	Can it be that he enjoys not for-long and should you then mad look-back that about son yours so well manned though that not praise all people for to-you his deeds".	It may be that he will not enjoy it for long, and then you will regret that your son is so well mannered, even though not all people praise you for his deeds".

2 | # 2 | # 2

Old Icelandic	Literal	English
En er á leið sumarið tók Þórhallur mjög að ógleðjast.	When was that passed summer took Thorhall much to ungladness.	When that summer was passed, Thorhall took much sadness.
Hallur spurði hví það sætti.	Hall asked what the reason.	Hall asked what the reason was.
Þórhallur svaraði:	Thorhall answered:	Thorhall answered:
"Illt hygg eg til haustboðs þessa er hér skal vera því að mér býður það fyrir að spámaður mun vera drepinn að þessi veislu".	"Ill think I to autumn-harvest this that here shall be for to me invited it for that a-seer shall be killed at this feast".	"I think evil of this autumn invitation which is to be here, for it offers me that a prophet will be killed at this feast".
"Þar kann eg að gera grein á", segir bóndi.	"Here can I that make explanation of", said the-farmer.	"I can explain that," said the farmer.
"Eg á uxa einn tíu vetra gamlan þann er eg kalla Spámann því að hann er spakari en flest naut önnur.	"I have ox one ten winters old that which I call The-Seer because that he is wiser than most bulls others.	"I have a ten-year-old ox, whom I call the Prophet, for he is wiser than most other bulls.

The Tale of Thiðrandi and Thórhall (Old Icelandic)

Old Icelandic	Literal	English
En hann skal drepa að haustboðinu og þarf þig þetta eigi að ógleðja því að eg ætla að þessi mín veisla sem aðrar skuli þér og öðrum vinum mínum verða til sæmdar".	But he shall be-killed at autumn-feast and need you this not be saddened because that I suppose that this my feast as others shall you and other friends mine be to honour".	But he will be killed at the autumn feast, and you need not be saddened because of this, for I think that this feast of mine, as well as others, will be an honour to you and to my other friends".
Þórhallur svarar:	Thorhall answered:	Thorhall answered:
"Eg fann þetta og eigi af því til að eg væri hræddur um mitt líf og boðar mér fyrir meiri tíðindi og undarlegri þau er eg mun að sinni eigi upp kveða".	"I found this and not of because to that I was scared about my life and proclaims to-me for greater tidings and stranger than is I may to mind not up speak".	"I found this not because I was afraid of my life, but because it proclaims to me more tidings and stranger ones that I have a mind not to speak up about".
Hallur mælti:	Hall said:	Hallur said:
"Þá er og ekki fyrir að bregða boði því".	"Then is and not for that break to-break therefore".	"Then there is no way to break the offer".
Þórhallur svarar:	Thorhall answered:	Þórhallur answered:
"Ekki mun það gera að mæla því að það mun fram ganga sem ætlað er".	"Not would that be that the-matter therefore that it should from going as intended be".	"It will not do in this matter because it will go as intended".
Veislan var búin að veturnóttum.	The-feast was prepared that winter-night.	The feast was prepared for the winter nights.
Kom þar fátt boðsmanna því að veður var hvasst og viðgerðarmikið.	Came there few invited-men because the weather was stormy and widely-made-much.	Few of the invited people came because the weather was stormy and difficult to travel in.
En er menn settust til borða um kveldið þá mælti Þórhallur:	When were the-people sat to the-tables about evening then spoke Thorhall:	When the people sat at the tables in the evening then Thorhall spoke:

The Tale of Thiðrandi and Thórhall (Old Icelandic)

Old Icelandic	Literal	English
"Biðja vildi eg að menn hefðu ráð mín um það að engi maður komi hér út á þessi nótt því að mikil mein munu hér á liggja ef af þessu er brugðið og hverigir hlutir sem verða í bendingum gefi menn eigi gaum að því, að illu mun furða ef nokkur ansar til".	"Ask will I that people have advice mine about it that no man comes here outside on this night for that much harm shall here to lay if of this is broken and whatever things which happen as signs give people not heed to for, that evil shall follow if anyone responds to".	"I wish to ask that people hear my advice that no man goes outside on this night, for there shall be much harm if this is broken and whatever things people might see as signs are to be given no heed to, for evil shall follow if anyone answers".
Hallur bað menn halda orð Þórhalls	Hall asked people hold words Thorhall's:	Hall asked people to hold to Thorhall's words:
"því að þau rjúfast ekki", segir hann,	"because that they break not", said he,	"because they will not break", he said,
"og er um heilt best að búa".	"and is about wholly best to prepare".	"and it will be best to be wholly prepared".
Þiðrandi gekk um beina.	Thidrandi went about assisting.	Thidrand went about assisting.
Var hann í því sem öðru mjúkur og lítillátur.	Was he as then as-in other-things humble and modest.	He was as in other things humble and modest.
En er menn gengu að sofa þá skipaði Þiðrandi gestum í sæng sína en hann sló sér niður í seti ystur við þili.	But when people went to sleep then directed Thidrandi guests to bed his but he laid-out himself down on a-bench outer with wall.	But when people went to sleep Thidrand directed guests to his bed and he laid himself down on a bench at the outermost wall.
En er flestir menn voru sofnaðir þá var kvatt dura og lét engi maður sem vissi.	When that most people were sleeping then was summons at-the-door and had no man as-if knew.	When most people were asleep there was a summons at the door, but no man acted as if they knew of it.
Fór svo þrisvar.	Came so three-times.	It came three times.
Þá spratt Þiðrandi upp og mælti:	Then sprang Thidrandi up and spoke:	Then Thidrand sprang up and spoke:
"Þetta er skömm mikil er menn láta hér allir sem sofi og munu boðsmenn komnir".	"This is a-shame great that people let here all who sleep and shall-be invited-men coming".	"This is a great shame that the people here are asleep and these must be guests coming".
Hann tók sverð í hönd sér og gekk út.	He took sword in hand his and went out.	He took his sword in his hand and went out.
Hann sá engan mann.	He saw no person.	He saw no person.

The Tale of Thiðrandi and Thórhall (Old Icelandic)

Old Icelandic	Literal	English
Honum kom þá það í hug að nokkurir boðsmenn mundu hafa riðið fyrir heim til bæjarins og riðið síðan aftur í móti þeim er seinna riðu.	To-him came then that a thought that some invited-men would have rode for the-house to the-town and rode afterwards back to meet them that later rode.	A thought came to him that some guests would have ridden to the house and then back to the town to meet those who had ridden behind them arriving later.
Hann gekk þá undir viðköstinn og heyrði að riðið var norðan á völlinn.	He went then under the-wood-pile and heard that riding was north into the-field.	He walked under the wood pile and heard the sound of riding coming from the north into the field.
Hann sá að það voru konur níu og voru allar í svörtum klæðum og höfðu brugðin sverð í höndum.	He saw that it was women nine and were all in black clothes and had drawn-out swords in hand.	He saw that there were nine women and they were all in black clothes and had drawn swords in their hands.
Hann heyrði og að riðið var sunnan á völlinn.	He heard also that riding was from-the-south into the-field.	He also heard the sound of riding coming from the south into the field.
Þar voru og níu konur, allar í ljósum klæðum og á hvítum hestum.	There were also nine women, all in bright clothes and on white horses.	There were also nine women, all in bright clothes and on white horses.
Þá vildi Þiðrandi snúa inn og segja mönnum sýnina en þá bar að konurnar fyrr, hinar svartklæddu, og sóttu að honum en hann varðist drengilega.	Then willed Thidrandi to-return inside and say-to the-men this-sight but then bore to the-women before, the black-clothes, and set-about to him and he defended bravely.	Then Thidrand wished to return inside and tell the men of what he had seen, but then the women in the black clothes came upon him first and set about him, and he defended himself bravely.

3

En langri stundu síðar vaknaði Þórhallur og spurði hvort Þiðrandi vekti og var honum eigi svarað.	Then a-long while later woke Thorhall and asked whether Thidrandi awoke and was he not answered.	A long while later Thorhall woke and asked whether Thidrand was awake but he was not answered.
Þórhallur kvað þá mundu ofseinað.	Thorhall cried then would-be too-late.	Thorhall cried out that it would be too late.
Var þá út gengið.	Were they out going.	They went outside.

The Tale of Thiðrandi and Thórhall (Old Icelandic)

Old Icelandic	Literal	English
Var á tunglskin og frostviðri.	Was it moonlight and frosty.	It was moonlight and frosty.
Þeir fundu Þiðranda liggja særðan og var hann borinn inn.	They found Thidrandi lying wounded and was he carried inside.	They found Thidrand lying wounded and was he carried inside.
Og er menn höfðu orð við hann sagði hann þetta allt sem fyrir hann hafði borið.	And when people had words with him told he this all that before he had bore.	And when the people had gotten word from him, he told them all that had happened before.
Hann andaðist þann sama morgun í lýsing og var lagður í haug að heiðnum sið.	He died that same morning at daybreak and was laid in a-mound as heathen tradition.	He died that same morning at daybreak and was laid in a mound as in the heathen tradition.
Síðan var haldið fréttum til um mannaferðir og vissu menn ekki vonir óvina Þiðranda.	Later was held news of about people's-travels and knew people not the-hopes enemies-of Thidrandi.	Later there was news of peoples' travels and people did not know the hopes of Thidrand's enemies.
Hallur spurði Þórhall hverju gegna mundi um þenna undarlega atburð.	Hall asked Thorhall how going would about these strange events.	Hall asked Thorhall how these strange events would turn out.
Þórhallur svarar:	Thorhall answered:	Thorhall answered:
"Það veit eg eigi en geta má eg til að þetta hafi engar konur verið aðrar en fylgjur yðrar frænda.	"That know I not but guess may I to that this have no women been other than followers your kinsmen.	"That I do not know, but I guess that these women can only have been followers of your kinsmen.
Get eg að hér eftir komi siðaskipti og mun því næst koma siður betri hingað til lands.	Guess I that here after comes conversion and should therefore next come a-custom better here to the-land.	I guess that there shall come a conversion, and there will be a better custom here to the land.
Ætla eg þær dísir yðrar er fylgt hafa þessum átrúnaði munu hafa vitað fyrir siðaskiptið og fyrir það að þér munuð verða þeim afhendir frændur.	Suppose I there spirits yours were followers having this religion would have known beforehand the-conversion and before it that you shall come-to them rejected kinsmen.	I suppose that these spirits of you who have followed the old faith would have known beforehand about this conversion, and that they would be rejected by your kinsmen.
Nú munu þær eigi hafa því unað að hafa engan skatt af yður áður og munu þær þetta hafa í sinn hlut.	Now shall they not have therefore liked to have no tribute from you before and would there that have in their lot.	Now they will not have liked to have had no tribute from you before and they would therefore have their lot.

The Tale of Thiðrandi and Thórhall (Old Icelandic)

Old Icelandic	Literal	English
En hinar betri dísir mundu vilja hjálpa honum og komust eigi við að svo búnu.	But the better spirits would will to-help him and they-came not with to so good.	But the better spirits would have wished to help him, but they did not arrive in time.
Nú munuð þér frændur þeirra njóta er þann munuð hafa er þær boða fyrir og fylgja".	Now shall you kinsmen of-them enjoy which then shall have what they preach for and follow".	Now your kinsmen shall enjoy the help of them by following what they preach for".
Nú boðaði þessi atburður fyrir sem Þórhallur sagði og margir hlutir þvílíkir þann fagnaðartíma sem eftir kom, að allsvaldandi guð virtist að líta miskunnaraugum á þann lýð er Ísland byggði og leysa það fólk fyrir sína erindreka af löngum fjandans þrældómi og leiða síðan til samlags eilífrar erfðar sinna æskilegra sona sem hann hefir fyrirheitið alla þá er honum vilja trúlega þjóna með staðfesti góðra verka.	Now foretold this event for which Thorhall said and many things like that celebrated-time which afterwards came, to omnipotent god seeming to look mercifully to that people of Iceland settled and redeemed that folk for their ambassadors of long damned slavery and lead afterwards to union eternal inherited his desirable sons whom he has fore-promised all those who him will truely serve with steadfast good works.	Now this event was foretold which Thorhall had said many things about, the celebrated time which came afterwards, an omnipotent god seeing and looking mercifully to the people that settled Iceland, redeeming the people from their ambassadors of long and damned slavery, leading afterwards to an eternal union, inherited by his desirable sons, that he has promised to all those who will truly serve him with steadfast good works.
Svo og eigi síður sýndi óvinur alls mannkyns opinberlega í slíkum hlutum og mörgum öðrum þeim er í frásagnir eru færðir hversu nauðigur hann lét laust sitt ránfengi og þann lýð er hann hafði áður allan tíma haldið hertekinn í villuböndum sinna bölvaðra skurðgoða þá er hann hvessti með slíkum áhlaupum sína grimmdarfulla reiði á þeim sem hann hafði vald yfir sem hann vissi nálgast sína skömm og maklegan skaða síns herfangs.	So and no less it-seemed enemies all mankind publicly in such things and many others they are of stories are told how compelled he to-have without this robbery and that people that he had before all time stayed captive of sins theirs cursed idols then when he hissed with such raids his cruelty-full anger at them which he had power over which he knew approached their shame and make-like damage his war-takings.	So and it seemed no less that the enemies of all mankind publicly and in such things and many others, of which there are stories told of how they were compelled to abandon robbery, and the people that had before remained captive of the sins of their cursed idols when they hissed with such brutality and cruelty-full anger at those which they had power over, of which they knew they approached their shame, and the damage of their war-takings.
En Halli þótti svo mikið lát Þiðranda sonar síns að hann undi eigi lengur að búa að Hofi.	But Hall thought so much had Thidrandi son his that he on not longer to live at Hof.	But Halli thought so much of his son Thidrand's death that he could no longer live at Hof.

The Tale of Thiðrandi and Thórhall (Old Icelandic)

Old Icelandic	Literal	English
Færði hann þá byggð sína til Þvottár.	Brought he then settlement his to Thvatta.	He then moved his settlement to Thvatta.
Það var einn tíma að Þvottá þá er Þórhallur spámaður var þar að heimboði með Halli.	It was one time at Thvatta then that Thorhall the-Seer was there at home-invitation with Hall.	There was a time at Thvatta when Thorhall the Seer was invited to stay with Hall.
Hallur lá í hvílugólfi og Þórhallur í annarri rekkju en gluggur var á hvílugólfinu.	Hall lay in bed-closet and Thorhall in another bed which window was on a-bed-closet.	Hall lay in a bed-closet and Thorhall in another bed-closet which had a window.
Og einn morgun er þeir vöktu báðir þá brosti Þórhallur.	And one morning when they woke both then burst-out-laughing Thorhall.	And one morning they both woke and then Thorhall burst out laughing.
Hallur mælti:	Hall spoke:	Hall spoke:
"Hví brosir þú nú?"	"Why laughing are-you now?"	"Why are you laughing now?"
Þórhallur svarar:	Thorhall answered:	Thorhall answered:
"Að því brosi eg að margur hóll opnast og hvert kvikvendi býr sinn bagga, bæði smá og stór, og gera fardaga".	"That because-of laughing am-I that many hills they-open and every creature prepares their bags, both small and great, and making moving-day".	"I am laughing because many hills are opening, and every creature prepares their bags, both small and great, and does their moving-day".
Og litlu síðar urðu þau tíðindi sem nú skal frá segja.	And little later came there the-news that now shall from be-said.	And a little while later there came the news that shall now be said from.

Word List *(Old Icelandic to English)*

Old Icelandic	English
A, a	
að	as, at, be, of, that, the, to
aðrar	other, others
aðrir	other
af	from, from, of, of
afhendir	rejected
aftur	back
aldur	age
alla	all
allan	all
allar	all
allir	all, all
allra	of-all
alls	all
allsvaldandi	omnipotent
allt	all
andaðist	died
annarri	another
ansar	responds
atburð	events
atburður	event
atgervi	deeds, deeds
atgervimaður	accomplished
austur	east, east
Á, á	
á	at, have, in, into, it, of, on, that, to
áður	before
áhlaupum	raids
álftafirði	Alftafjord (place)
átján	eighteen
átrúnaði	religion
Æ, æ	
ærin	mad
æskilegra	desirable
ætla	suppose
ætlað	intended
B, b	
bað	asked
báðir	both
bæði	both
bæjarins	the-town
bagga	bags
bar	bore
barn	child
bauð	invited
beina	assisting
bendingum	signs
ber	bears
berufirði	Berufjord (place)
best	best
betri	better
biðja	ask
bjó	settled
blíðskap	kindness
blíður	gentle
boða	preach
boðaði	foretold
boðar	proclaims
boði	to-break
boðsmanna	invited-men
boðsmenn	invited-men
bölvaðra	cursed
bóndi	the-farmer
borða	the-tables
borið	bore
borinn	carried
bregða	break
brosi	laughing
brosir	laughing
brosti	burst-out-laughing
brugðið	broken
brugðin	drawn-out
búa	live, prepare
búin	prepared

37

Word List (Old Icelandic to English)

Old Icelandic	English
búnu	good
býður	invited
byggð	settlement
byggði	settled
býr	prepares

D, d

Old Icelandic	English
dáðust	admired
dísir	spirits
dögum	the-days-of
drengilega	bravely
drepa	be-killed
drepinn	killed
dura	at-the-door
dvaldist	dwelled

E, e

Old Icelandic	English
eða	or, or-that
ef	if
efnilegastur	promising
eftir	after, afterwards
eftirsjá	look-back
eg	am-I, I
eigi	no, not
eilífrar	eternal
einn	one
eitt	one
ekki	not
elsti	eldest
en	and, but, than, then, when, which
engan	no
engar	no
engi	no
enn	as
er	are, as, be, is, of, that, that-which, was, were, what, when, which, who
erfðar	inherited
erindreka	ambassadors
eru	are

F, f

Old Icelandic	English
færði	brought
færðir	told
fagnaðartíma	celebrated-time
fann	found
fara	travel
fardaga	moving-day
fátt	few
fjandans	damned
flest	most
flestir	most
föður	father
fólk	folk
fór	came, travelled
frá	from
frænda	kinsmen
frændur	kinsmen
fram	from
framsýnn	far-sighted
frásagnir	stories
fréttum	news
fróður	a-wise
frostviðri	frosty
fundu	found
furða	follow
fylgja	follow
fylgjur	followers
fylgt	followers
fyrir	before, beforehand, for
fyrirheitið	fore-promised
fyrr	before
fyrri	before

G, g

Old Icelandic	English
gamlan	old
ganga	going
gaum	heed
gefi	give
gegna	going
gekk	went

Word List (Old Icelandic to English)

Old Icelandic	English
gengið	going
gengu	went
gengur	goes
gera	be, make, making
gestum	guests
get	guess
geta	guess
gisti	guested
gluggur	window
góðra	good
grein	explanation
grimmdarfulla	cruelty-full
guð	god

H, h

Old Icelandic	English
hafa	have, having
hafði	had
hafi	have
hákonar	Hakon (name)
halda	hold
haldið	held, stayed
halli	Hall (name)
halls	Hall's (name)
hallur	Hall (name)
hann	he, him
hans	he, his
haug	a-mound
haustboði	autumn-feast
haustboðinu	autumn-feast
haustboðs	autumn-harvest
hefðu	have
hefir	has
heiðnum	heathen
heilt	wholly
heim	home, the-house
heimboða	home-invitation
heimboði	home-invitation
heldur	but
hér	here
herfangs	war-takings
hertekinn	captive
hestum	horses
hét	was-named
heyrði	heard

Old Icelandic	English
hin	the
hinar	the
hingað	here
hinn	most, the, the-most
hinum	the
hitt	others
hjálpa	to-help
hlut	lot
hluti	things
hlutir	things
hlutum	things
hlutur	part
höfðu	had
hofi	Hof (place)
hóll	hills
hönd	hand
höndum	hand
honum	he, him, to-him
hörgslandi	Horgsland (place)
hræddur	scared
hug	thought
hvar	where
hvasst	stormy
hverigir	whatever
hverju	how
hversu	how
hvert	each, every
hvessti	hissed
hví	what, why
hvílugólfi	bed-closet
hvílugólfinu	a-bed-closet
hvítum	white
hvort	whether
hygg	think

I, i

Old Icelandic	English
illt	ill
illu	evil
inn	inside

Word List (Old Icelandic to English)

Old Icelandic	English

Í, í

í	a, as, at, in, of, on, to
ísland	Iceland (place)
íslands	Iceland (place)

J, j

jafnan	always, usual
jarls	the-earl

K, k

kalla	call
kallaður	called
kann	can
klæðum	clothes
kom	came
koma	come
komi	comes
komnir	coming
komust	they-came
konur	women
konurnar	the-women
kvað	cried
kvatt	summons
kveða	speak
kveldið	evening
kvikvendi	creature

L, l

lá	lay
lagður	laid
land	land
landa	the-lands
lands	the-land
langri	a-long
lát	had
láta	let
laust	without
leið	passed
leiða	lead
lengi	for-long
lengur	longer
lét	had, to-have
leysa	redeemed
líf	life
liggja	lay, lying
líta	look
lítillátur	modest
lítils	little
litlu	little
ljósum	bright
lofa	praise
lofi	praise
lofuðu	praised
lokið	ended
löngum	long
lýð	people
lýsing	daybreak

M, m

má	may
maður	a-man, man
mæla	the-matter
mælir	say
mælti	said, spoke, spoke
maklegan	make-like
mann	person
manna	a-man
mannaðan	manned
mannaferðir	people's-travels
mannkyns	mankind
marga	many
margir	many
margur	many
með	with
mein	harm
meiri	greater
menn	people, the-people
mér	I, me, to-me
merkilegasti	remarkable
merkilegt	remarkable
mest	the-most
mesta	greatest, most

Word List (Old Icelandic to English)

Old Icelandic	English
mesti	most
mikið	much
mikil	great, much
milli	between
mín	mine, my
mínum	mine
miskunnaraugum	mercifully
mislíki	mislike
mitt	my
mjög	much
mjúkur	humble
mönnum	the-men
mörgum	many
morgun	morning
móti	meet
mun	may, shall, should, would
mundi	would
mundu	would, would-be
munu	shall, shall-be, would
munuð	shall

N, n

Old Icelandic	English
næst	next
nálgast	approached
nauðigur	compelled
naut	bulls
niður	down
níu	nine
njóta	enjoy
njóti	enjoys
nokkur	anyone, some
nokkurir	some
nokkuru	sometime
norðan	north
norrænn	northern
nótt	night
nú	now

O, o

Old Icelandic	English
ofseinað	too-late
oft	often
og	also, and
opinberlega	publicly
opnast	they-open
orð	words

Ó, ó

Old Icelandic	English
ógleðja	saddened
ógleðjast	ungladness
óvina	enemies-of
óvinur	enemies

Ö, ö

Old Icelandic	English
öðru	other-things
öðrum	other, others
önnur	others

R, r

Old Icelandic	English
ráð	advice
ránfengi	robbery
reið	rode, was-riding
reiði	anger
rekkju	bed
riðið	riding, rode
riðu	rode
rjúfast	break

S, s

Old Icelandic	English
sá	saw
sæmdar	honour
sæng	bed
særðan	wounded
sætti	reason
sagði	said, said, told

Word List (Old Icelandic to English)

Old Icelandic	English	Old Icelandic	English
sama	same	sonar	son
samlags	union	sonur	son
segir	said	sóttu	set-about
segja	be-said, say-to	spakari	wiser
seinna	later	spámaður	a-seer, the-Seer
sem	as, as-if, as-in, that, which, who, whom	spámann	the-Seer
sér	himself, his	spratt	sprang
seti	a-bench	spurði	asked
settust	sat	staðfesti	steadfast
sið	tradition	stór	great
síðan	afterwards, later	stundu	while
síðar	later	sumar	summer
siðaskipti	conversion	sumarið	summer
siðaskiptið	the-conversion	sunnan	from-the-south
síðu-hallur	Sidu-Hall (name)	svarað	answered
siður	a-custom	svaraði	answered
síður	less	svarar	answered
sig	himself	svartklæddu	black-clothes
sigurðarsonar	Sigurdson (name)	sverð	sword, swords
sína	his, their	svo	so
sinn	their	svörtum	black
sinna	his, theirs	sýndi	it-seemed
sinni	mind	sýnina	this-sight
síns	his	sýrlækjarósi	Syrlaekjaros (place)
sínum	his		
sitt	this		
sjái	see		
sjálfur	of-himself		
skaða	damage		

T, t

skal	shall	tíðindi	the-news, tidings
skatt	tribute	til	of, to, until
skipaði	directed	tíma	time
skömm	a-shame, shame	tíu	ten
skuli	shall	tók	took
skurðgoða	idols	trúlega	truely
skyldi	should	tunglskin	moonlight

Þ, þ

slíkum	such		
sló	laid-out		
smá	small	þá	then, they, those
snúa	to-return	það	it, that, the
sofa	sleep	þær	there, they
sofi	sleep	þagði	silent
sofnaðir	sleeping	þangað	from-there
son	son	þann	that, that, then
sona	sons	þar	here, there

42

Word List (Old Icelandic to English)

Old Icelandic	English
þarf	need
þau	than, there, they
þegar	once
þeim	them, they
þeir	they
þeirra	of-them
þenna	these
þér	to-you, you
þess	this
þessa	this
þessi	this
þessu	this
þessum	this
þetta	that, this
þiðranda	Thidrandi (name)
þiðrandi	Thidrandi (name)
þig	you
þili	wall
þingi	the-assembly
þings	the-assembly
þinn	yours
þjóna	serve
þó	although, though
þórhall	Thorhall (name)
þórhalli	Thorhall (name)
þórhalls	Thorhall's (name)
þórhallur	Thorhall (name)
þótti	thought
þrældómi	slavery
þrisvar	three-times
þú	are-you, you
því	because, because-of, for, then, therefore
þvílíkir	like
þvottá	Thvatta (place)
þvottár	Thvatta (place)
þykir	think

U, u

um	about
unað	liked
undarlega	strange
undarlegri	stranger
undi	on
undir	under
unni	loved
upp	up
urðu	came
uxa	ox

Ú, ú

út	out, outside

V, v

vænstur	handsome
væri	the-home, was
vaknaði	woke
vald	power
var	was, were
varðist	defended
veður	weather
veisla	feast
veislan	the-feast
veislu	feast
veit	know
vekti	awoke
vel	well
vera	be
verða	be, become, come-to, happen
verið	been
verka	works
vetra	winters
veturnóttum	winter-night
við	with
viðgerðarmikið	widely-made-much
viðköstinn	the-wood-pile
vildi	will, willed
vilja	will
villuböndum	sins
vin	friend
vinátta	friendship
vinsælasti	endearing
vinum	friends
virði	values
virtist	seeming

Word List (Old Icelandic to English)

Old Icelandic	English
vissi	knew
vissu	knew
vitað	known
vöktu	woke
völlinn	the-field
vonir	the-hopes
voru	was, were

Y, y

yðrar	your, yours
yður	you
yfir	over
ystur	outer

Word List *(English to Old Icelandic)*

English	Old Icelandic	English	Old Icelandic
A, a		at-the-door	*dura*
		autumn-feast	*haustboði, haustboðinu*
a	*í*	autumn-harvest	*haustboðs*
a-bed-closet	*hvílugólfinu*	a-wise	*fróður*
a-bench	*seti*	awoke	*vekti*
about	*um*		
accomplished	*atgervimaður*	**B, b**	
a-custom	*siður*		
admired	*dáðust*	back	*aftur*
advice	*ráð*	bags	*bagga*
after	*eftir*	be	*að, er, gera, vera, verða*
afterwards	*eftir, síðan*	bears	*ber*
age	*aldur*	because	*því*
Alftafjord (place)	*álftafirði*	because-of	*því*
all	*alla, allan, allar, allir, alls, allt*	become	*verða*
a-long	*langri*	bed	*rekkju, sæng*
also	*og*	bed-closet	*hvílugólfi*
although	*þó*	been	*verið*
always	*jafnan*	before	*áður, fyrir, fyrr, fyrri*
a-man	*maður, manna*	beforehand	*fyrir*
ambassadors	*erindreka*	be-killed	*drepa*
am-I	*eg*	Berufjord (place)	*berufirði*
a-mound	*haug*	be-said	*segja*
and	*en, og*	best	*best*
anger	*reiði*	better	*betri*
another	*annarri*	between	*milli*
answered	*svarað, svaraði, svarar*	black	*svörtum*
anyone	*nokkur*	black-clothes	*svartklæddu*
approached	*nálgast*	bore	*bar, borið*
are	*er, eru*	both	*báðir, bæði*
are-you	*þú*	bravely	*drengilega*
as	*að, enn, er, í, sem*	break	*bregða, rjúfast*
a-seer	*spámaður*	bright	*ljósum*
a-shame	*skömm*	broken	*brugðið*
as-if	*sem*	brought	*færði*
as-in	*sem*	bulls	*naut*
ask	*biðja*	burst-out-laughing	*brosti*
asked	*bað, spurði*	but	*en, heldur*
assisting	*beina*		
at	*á, að, í*		

Word List (English to Old Icelandic)

English	Old Icelandic

C, c

call	kalla
called	kallaður
came	fór, kom, urðu
can	kann
captive	hertekinn
carried	borinn
celebrated-time	fagnaðartíma
child	barn
clothes	klæðum
come	koma
comes	komi
come-to	verða
coming	komnir
compelled	nauðigur
conversion	siðaskipti
creature	kvikvendi
cried	kvað
cruelty-full	grimmdarfulla
cursed	bölvaðra

D, d

damage	skaða
damned	fjandans
daybreak	lýsing
deeds	atgervi
defended	varðist
desirable	æskilegra
died	andaðist
directed	skipaði
down	niður
drawn-out	brugðin
dwelled	dvaldist

E, e

each	hvert
east	austur
eighteen	átján
eldest	elsti
endearing	vinsælasti
ended	lokið
enemies	óvinur
enemies-of	óvina
enjoy	njóta
enjoys	njóti
eternal	eilífrar
evening	kveldið
event	atburður
events	atburð
every	hvert
evil	illu
explanation	grein

F, f

far-sighted	framsýnn
father	föður
feast	veisla, veislu
few	fátt
folk	fólk
follow	furða, fylgja
followers	fylgjur, fylgt
for	fyrir, því
fore-promised	fyrirheitið
foretold	boðaði
for-long	lengi
found	fann, fundu
friend	vin
friends	vinum
friendship	vinátta
from	af, frá, fram
from-there	þangað
from-the-south	sunnan
frosty	frostviðri

G, g

gentle	blíður
give	gefi
god	guð
goes	gengur
going	ganga, gegna, gengið
good	búnu, góðra
great	mikil, stór

Word List (English to Old Icelandic)

English	*Old Icelandic*	English	*Old Icelandic*
greater	*meiri*		
greatest	*mesta*		
guess	*get, geta*		
guested	*gisti*		
guests	*gestum*		

H, h

I, i

English	*Old Icelandic*
had	*hafði, höfðu, lát, lét*
Hakon (name)	*hákonar*
Hall (name)	*halli, hallur*
Hall's (name)	*halls*
hand	*hönd, höndum*
handsome	*vænstur*
happen	*verða*
harm	*mein*
has	*hefir*
have	*á, hafa, hafi, hefðu*
having	*hafa*
he	*hann, hans, honum*
heard	*heyrði*
heathen	*heiðnum*
heed	*gaum*
held	*haldið*
here	*hér, hingað, þar*
hills	*hóll*
him	*hann, honum*
himself	*sér, sig*
his	*hans, sér, sína, sinna, síns, sínum*
hissed	*hvessti*
Hof (place)	*hofi*
hold	*halda*
home	*heim*
home-invitation	*heimboða, heimboði*
honour	*sæmdar*
Horgsland (place)	*hörgslandi*
horses	*hestum*
how	*hverju, hversu*
humble	*mjúkur*

English	*Old Icelandic*
I	*eg, mér*
Iceland (place)	*ísland, íslands*
idols	*skurðgoða*
if	*ef*
ill	*illt*
in	*á, í*
inherited	*erfðar*
inside	*inn*
intended	*ætlað*
into	*á*
invited	*bauð, býður*
invited-men	*boðsmanna, boðsmenn*
is	*er*
it	*á, það*
it-seemed	*sýndi*

K, k

English	*Old Icelandic*
killed	*drepinn*
kindness	*blíðskap*
kinsmen	*frænda, frændur*
knew	*vissi, vissu*
know	*veit*
known	*vitað*

L, l

English	*Old Icelandic*
laid	*lagður*
laid-out	*sló*
land	*land*
later	*seinna, síðan, síðar*
laughing	*brosi, brosir*
lay	*lá, liggja*
lead	*leiða*
less	*síður*
let	*láta*
life	*líf*
like	*þvílíkir*
liked	*unað*
little	*lítils, litlu*

Word List (English to Old Icelandic)

English	Old Icelandic	English	Old Icelandic
live	búa	no	eigi, engan, engar, engi
long	löngum	north	norðan
longer	lengur	northern	norrænn
look	líta	not	eigi, ekki
look-back	eftirsjá	now	nú
lot	hlut		
loved	unni		
lying	liggja		

M, m

O, o

English	Old Icelandic	English	Old Icelandic
mad	ærin	of	á, að, af, er, í, til
make	gera	of-all	allra
make-like	maklegan	of-himself	sjálfur
making	gera	often	oft
man	maður	of-them	þeirra
mankind	mannkyns	old	gamlan
manned	mannaðan	omnipotent	allsvaldandi
many	marga, margir, margur, mörgum	on	á, í, undi
may	má, mun	once	þegar
me	mér	one	einn, eitt
meet	móti	or	eða
mercifully	miskunnaraugum	or-that	eða
mind	sinni	other	aðrar, aðrir, öðrum
mine	mín, mínum	others	aðrar, hitt, öðrum, önnur
mislike	mislíki	other-things	öðru
modest	lítillátur	out	út
moonlight	tunglskin	outer	ystur
morning	morgun	outside	út
most	flest, flestir, hinn, mesta, mesti	over	yfir
moving-day	fardaga	ox	uxa
much	mikið, mikil, mjög		
my	mín, mitt		

N, n

P, p

English	Old Icelandic	English	Old Icelandic
need	þarf	part	hlutur
news	fréttum	passed	leið
next	næst	people	lýð, menn
night	nótt	people's-travels	mannaferðir
nine	níu	person	mann
		power	vald
		praise	lofa, lofi
		praised	lofuðu
		preach	boða
		prepare	búa
		prepared	búin

Word List (English to Old Icelandic)

English	*Old Icelandic*	English	*Old Icelandic*
prepares	*býr*	sins	*villuböndum*
proclaims	*boðar*	slavery	*þrældómi*
promising	*efnilegastur*	sleep	*sofa, sofi*
publicly	*opinberlega*	sleeping	*sofnaðir*
		small	*smá*
		so	*svo*
		some	*nokkur, nokkurir*
		sometime	*nokkuru*

R, r

		son	*son, sonar, sonur*
raids	*áhlaupum*	sons	*sona*
reason	*sætti*	speak	*kveða*
redeemed	*leysa*	spirits	*dísir*
rejected	*afhendir*	spoke	*mælti*
religion	*átrúnaði*	sprang	*spratt*
remarkable	*merkilegasti, merkilegt*	stayed	*haldið*
		steadfast	*staðfesti*
responds	*ansar*	stories	*frásagnir*
riding	*riðið*	stormy	*hvasst*
robbery	*ránfengi*	strange	*undarlega*
rode	*reið, riðið, riðu*	stranger	*undarlegri*
		such	*slíkum*
		summer	*sumar, sumarið*

S, s

		summons	*kvatt*
saddened	*ógleðja*	suppose	*ætla*
said	*mælti, sagði, segir*	sword	*sverð*
same	*sama*	swords	*sverð*
sat	*settust*	Syrlaekjaros (place)	*sýrlækjarósi*
saw	*sá*		
say	*mælir*		

T, t

say-to	*segja*		
scared	*hræddur*	ten	*tíu*
see	*sjái*	than	*en, þau*
seeming	*virtist*	that	*á, að, er, sem, það, þann, þetta*
serve	*þjóna*		
set-about	*sóttu*	that-which	*er*
settled	*bjó, byggði*	the	*að, hin, hinar, hinn, hinum, það*
settlement	*byggð*		
shall	*mun, munu, munuð, skal, skuli*	the-assembly	*þingi, þings*
		the-conversion	*siðaskiptið*
shall-be	*munu*	the-days-of	*dögum*
shame	*skömm*	the-earl	*jarls*
should	*mun, skyldi*	the-farmer	*bóndi*
Sidu-Hall (name)	*síðu-hallur*	the-feast	*veislan*
signs	*bendingum*	the-field	*völlinn*
Sigurdson (name)	*sigurðarsonar*	the-home	*væri*
silent	*þagði*		

Word List (English to Old Icelandic)

English	Old Icelandic
the-hopes	vonir
the-house	heim
their	sína, sinn
theirs	sinna
the-land	lands
the-lands	landa
them	þeim
the-matter	mæla
the-men	mönnum
the-most	hinn, mest
then	en, þá, þann, því
the-news	tíðindi
the-people	menn
there	þær, þar, þau
therefore	því
these	þenna
the-Seer	spámaður, spámann
the-tables	borða
the-town	bæjarins
the-women	konurnar
the-wood-pile	viðköstinn
they	þá, þær, þau, þeim, þeir
they-came	komust
they-open	opnast
Thidrandi (name)	þiðranda, þiðrandi
things	hluti, hlutir, hlutum
think	hygg, þykir
this	sitt, þess, þessa, þessi, þessu, þessum, þetta
this-sight	sýnina
Thorhall (name)	þórhall, þórhalli, þórhallur
Thorhall's (name)	þórhalls
those	þá
though	þó
thought	hug, þótti
three-times	þrisvar
Thvatta (place)	þvottá, þvottár
tidings	tíðindi
time	tíma
to	á, að, í, til
to-break	boði
to-have	lét
to-help	hjálpa
to-him	honum
told	færðir, sagði
to-me	mér
took	tók
too-late	ofseinað
to-return	snúa
to-you	þér
tradition	sið
travel	fara
travelled	fór
tribute	skatt
truely	trúlega

U, u

English	Old Icelandic
under	undir
ungladness	ógleðjast
union	samlags
until	til
up	upp
usual	jafnan

V, v

English	Old Icelandic
values	virði

W, w

English	Old Icelandic
wall	þili
war-takings	herfangs
was	er, væri, var, voru
was-named	hét
was-riding	reið
weather	veður
well	vel
went	gekk, gengu
were	er, var, voru
what	er, hví
whatever	hverigir
when	en, er
where	hvar
whether	hvort
which	en, er, sem

Word List (English to Old Icelandic)

English	Old Icelandic
while	*stundu*
white	*hvítum*
who	*er, sem*
wholly	*heilt*
whom	*sem*
why	*hví*
widely-made-much	*viðgerðarmikið*
will	*vildi, vilja*
willed	*vildi*
window	*gluggur*
winter-night	*veturnóttum*
winters	*vetra*
wiser	*spakari*
with	*með, við*
without	*laust*
woke	*vaknaði, vöktu*
women	*konur*
words	*orð*
works	*verka*
would	*mun, mundi, mundu, munu*
would-be	*mundu*
wounded	*særðan*

Y, y

you	*þér, þig, þú, yður*
your	*yðrar*
yours	*þinn, yðrar*

A Word Comparison of Old Norse and Old Icelandic Words

Old Norse	Old Icelandic	English	Old Norse	Old Icelandic	English
áðr	áður	before	frændr	frændur	kinsmen
ætlat	ætlað	intended	fróðr	fróður	a-wise
aftr	aftur	back	fyrr	fyrir	for
aldr	aldur	age	gengit	gengið	going
anzar	ansar	responds	gengr	gengur	goes
at	að	as	gera	að	that
at	að	at	gkal	skal	shall
at	að	be	gluggr	gluggur	window
at	að	of	grimdarfulla	grimmdarfulla	cruelty-full
at	að	that	guði	guð	god
at	að	the	hafa	vilja	will
at	að	to	haft	þetta	that
at	gera	be	haldit	haldið	held
atburðr	atburður	event	haldit	haldið	stayed
atgervismaðr	atgervimaður	accomplished	hallr	hallur	Hall (name)
austr	austur	east	hefði	hefðu	have
berr	ber	bears	heldr	heldur	but
bezt	best	best	hin	hinum	the
blíðr	blíður	gentle	hingat	hingað	here
bœjar	bæjarins	the-town	hlutr	hlutur	part
bölvuðu	bölvaðra	cursed	hræddr	hræddur	scared
borit	borið	bore	hvárt	hvort	whether
brugðit	brugðið	broken	kallaðr	kallaður	called
býðr	býður	invited	kveldit	kveldið	evening
drengiliga	drengilega	bravely	kvikindi	kvikvendi	creature
dyra	dura	at-the-door	lagðr	lagður	laid
eðr	eða	or	lengr	lengur	longer
eðr	eða	or-that	lítillátr	lítillátur	modest
efniligastr	efnilegastur	promising	lokit	lokið	ended
eigi	ekki	not	maðr	maður	a-man
ek	eg	am-I	maðr	maður	man
ek	eg	I	makligan	maklegan	make-like
elzti	elsti	eldest	margr	margur	many
enn	en	and	mikit	mikið	much
enn	en	but	mjök	mjög	much
enn	en	than	mjúkr	mjúkur	humble
enn	en	then	morgin	morgun	morning
enn	en	when	mundri	mundu	would
enn	en	which	munit	munuð	shall
fœrði	færði	brought	munut	munuð	shall
fœrðir	færðir	told	myndi	mundi	would

A Word Comparison of Old Norse and Old Icelandic

Old Norse	Old Icelandic	English
myndi	mundu	would
nauðigr	nauðigur	compelled
niðr	niður	down
nökkurir	nokkurir	some
nökkurr	nokkur	anyone
nökkurr	nokkur	some
nökkuru	nokkuru	sometime
norrœnn	norrænn	northern
œrin	ærin	mad
œskilegra	æskilegra	desirable
of	ofseinað	too-late
ok	og	also
ok	og	and
opinberliga	opinberlega	publicly
óvinr	óvinur	enemies
riðit	riðið	riding
riðit	riðið	rode
sæti	seti	a-bench
siðaskifti	siðaskipti	conversion
siðaskifti	siðaskiptið	the-conversion
siðr	siður	a-custom
síðr	síður	less
síðu-hallr	síðu-hallur	Sidu-Hall (name)
sik	sig	himself
sjálfr	sjálfur	of-himself
sœmdar	sæmdar	honour
sonr	sonur	son
spámaðr	spámaður	a-seer
spámaðr	spámaður	the-Seer
sumarit	sumarið	summer
svá	svo	so
svarar	svaraði	answered
svarat	svarað	answered
sýrlœkjarósi	sýrlækjarósi	Syrlaekjaros (place)
þangat	þangað	from-there
þar	það	that
þat	mæla	the-matter
þat	það	it
þat	það	that
þat	það	the
þeira	þeirra	of-them
þik	þig	you

Old Norse	Old Icelandic	English
þórhallr	þórhallur	Thorhall (name)
þváttá	þvottá	Thvatta (place)
þváttár	þvottár	Thvatta (place)
þykkir	þykir	think
tjóa	það	that
unat	unað	liked
undarliga	undarlega	strange
undarligri	undarlegri	stranger
vænstr	vænstur	handsome
væra	væri	was
vánir	vonir	the-hopes
varu	voru	was
váru	voru	were
veðr	veður	weather
veizla	veisla	feast
veizlan	veislan	the-feast
veizlu	veislu	feast
verit	verið	been
vetrnóttum	veturnóttum	winter-night
viðgerðarmikit	viðgerðarmikið	widely-made-much
vilda	vildi	will
virðist	virtist	seeming
vitat	vitað	known
yðr	yður	you
yztr	ystur	outer